Everybody's Vaguely Familiar

Praise for *Everybody's Vaguely Familiar*:

I love Jack Powers' light touch and deep vision. *Everybody's Vaguely Familiar* is brilliant, humanistic, quick-witted and fast-paced — but the cameos of family, high school, pop icons and suburbia open seamlessly onto the sacred ground of tragedy: mortality, suffering, how we create ourselves out of nothing and are undone. In "Smokin' a Real Cool Brank," Powers' zinging lines arrive at an epiphany — "an acute awareness of my good fortune" — but that's not where the poem ends: it ends in the human predicament: illusion, desire, cussedness, our need to flirt with disaster. *Everybody's Vaguely Familiar* is a book that will last.

— D. Nurkse

The poems in Jack Powers' debut collection, *Everybody's Vaguely Familiar* are as human as it gets, maneuvering through the emotional landscape of life with wit, a no-nonsense clarity and a touch of sarcasm. These poems are immediate, as if each one is talking specifically to you, the reader, creating a bridge of instant friendship. So when Powers explores fatherhood, the death of a parent, or how we can get the most out of the time we do have, his poems offer a past, present and most importantly a future. Read this collection and celebrate what it means to be alive.

— Kevin Pilkington

Everybody's Vaguely Familiar is a funny and poignant ride through the vivid details of our everyday lives. From adolescent smoking to philtrum guards to a miscarriage, Powers captures a male voice in search of what it all adds up to — if anything. In this carefully observant collection, he appears to suggest that even though we fail the ones we love and death claims us all, the struggle is worth it, especially when family shares it with us: "I will ... /remember a beach in Rhodes// where stars littered the sky/ like luminescent river stones/ so close// we could pluck them/ from the heavens,/ offer them to each other...." Powers' book shows us how to "wish for more."

— Laurel Peterson

Jack Powers is atuned to twists of life and language — insults refitted as endearments, families defined by their troubles, great care taken with modes of recklessness, and in his deftly funny title poem, *Everybody's Vaguely Familiar*, remembering people while forgetting faces. At the start of his debut collection, he's praising the massive coronary, favoring it over the dwindling disease and dementia that took his elders. But as mortality hovers, he teases, testing wits and pulling out the good stories of lucky close calls, game grandmothers, swearing babies, and a wry mother's sartorial ghosting of her son. Pretty soon, he's against the quick demise — "and the sky seemed full/ of answers, some hurtling/like arrows into the future."

— Amy Holman

Jack Powers' powerful debut collection grapples with existential questions of death, illness, and love. Yet it is one of the most life-affirming collections I have read. Powers' precision of language, his enormous empathy, and his razor-sharp sense of humor allow him to walk the treacherous tightrope of sentiment without ever falling into the abyss of sentimentality. He makes the reader care passionately about the quotidian troubles of his characters. Powers' command of language and his unique voice offer a profound and affecting glimpse of dashed dreams; boyhood exploits; a miscarriage; dementia; deaths of parents, students, friends; and a unique brush with death at age twenty-nine. The persona is as nuanced as the character in a novel. This collection lives at the intersection between the dueling world-views of the book — "In Praise of Heart Attacks" and "In Fear of Heart Attacks." While reading this engaging collection, the reader ultimately understands that despite the arguments Powers posits in favor of a swift and painless death, life with all its disappointments and heartaches is undeniably gratifying. This book reminds me how grateful I am to be alive.

— Jennifer Franklin

Everybody's Vaguely Familiar

Poems

Jack Powers

Golden Antelope Press
715 E. McPherson
Kirksville, Missouri 63501
2018

ISBN: 978-1-936135-63-9

Library of Congress Control Number: 2018956547

Published by:
Golden Antelope Press
715 E. McPherson
Kirksville, Missouri 63501

Available at:
Golden Antelope Press
715 E. McPherson
Kirksville, Missouri, 63501
Phone: (660) 665-0273
http://www.goldenantelope.com
Email: ndelmoni@gmail.com

Author's Note

Writing a poem is an act of self-indulgence and generosity – depending on the day and the poem. So I'd like to first thank you, dear reader, for reading these poems. I hope it's a generous day.

I'd also like to thank the whole village of idiots who have supported, encouraged and humored me throughout this process starting with my parents who gave me lots of material to work with. And thanks to my siblings, Chris, Donny and Ellen, and to my children, Zak, Erin and Will, who make many appearances here – sometimes against their will – and have helped shape many poems; to my mother-in-law, Joan Kester Armstrong, who was an unwitting patron for many years; to co-founder Del Shortliffe, current members Bill McCarthy, Nicole Garcia, Bob Darken and all the other teachers in my CWP writing group of 33 years for the deadlines and feedback and laughter.

And thanks to my wise and generous professors at Sarah Lawrence, especially Joan Larkin and Marie Howe who led me to believe I could hang with the poets – as well as Laure Anne Bosselaar, Thomas Lux, Stephen Dobyns and Mark Wunderlich who showed me the ropes and encouraged me to become stranger in my own way and Dennis Nurkse who patiently helped me put together the thesis which was the first, long-ago draft of this book; to the many teachers along the way, including Terrance Hayes, Martha Rhodes and Kathryn Nuernberger to name just a few; to Laurel, Van and Carol of my Norwalk writing group who helped me shape this into a workable draft; to Amy Holman who helped me revise and find a publisher; to Jennifer Franklin and her Year of the Book class who helped me revise some more; to my editors, Betsy and Neal Delmonico, who believed enough to publish this; and most of all to my wife Anne who has sacrificed decades of days and nights so I could live this fantasy. I thank and blame you all.

Contents

I

Bonehead

My mother signed notes in my high school lunch bag,
Love, Bonehead, long after we could talk of love.
She laughed at the sound of the word, the cartoon image.
And *Love* elevated *Bonehead* to a tender ache
that reached across the gap from weary mother to leery teen.
She hated *lousy* and *meal*, but to her *bonehead*
sounded gentler than *idiot, dope, moron, cretin* – although
dope acquired a softness when my father,
deep in his dementia, asked, after a long day of song
and cake and tears for my five year old, *Whose birthday is it?*
And my mom, a skeleton herself after a year and a half
of waking to find him dressed in three polo shirts
on damp July nights or hiding the markers so he'd stop
writing names on the photos of the grandchildren, said,
It's Will's, ya dope, and we all laughed at the exhausted
appropriateness. Too tired for *Bonehead*, she took it
up a notch and we all appropriated the word to use
when loved ones wore us down to the bone.

In Praise of Heart Attacks

Not the sneaky kind at forty when your kids are seven and nine.
Not the cheap ones that fence you into smaller and smaller yards.
I'm talking massive coronary in the late 70's – 82 tops.
Here to *not here* in an instant. I've seen a mind go slowly
from What was I saying? to How did we get here?
to There's a woman in our room trying to dress me.
Not for me: body dwindling from walking to walker to waiting
and wheezing. Slow decline into silence? Uh uh.
No sir. A massive stroke would do. Something sudden
and self-contained. No clean up. You're thinking it's bad luck
to say aloud. Or bad form. It's cruel to the survivors.
                                        No. Survivors
wipe your drool and your ass, try to remember who you were.
They should thank me. You think I'll chicken out? Maybe.
Maybe in the end, something's better than nothing.
But if there's a button I can push, I'm buying. So at let's say 78,
stop the Coumadin, the Heparin, the Beta Blockers,
the latest magic pill. No more static. Let the heart know
when it's time to go. Say farewell. Let's end this show on time.

The God of Stupidity

I'm on the roof of Buzzy's car, spread-eagled for grip,
fingernails dug into the rubber seal around the windshield,
eyes tearing from the cold rain-specked wind coming at me.

Buzzy turns on the wipers – I had dared him to knock me off.
But I've learned not to flinch. The lake is somewhere off to the north.
We've just left The Rongovian Embassy, perhaps forcibly,

after a marriage ceremony improvised with tequila, a juke box
of country songs and a smattering of invented Rongovian
with a girl I'd met that night – Linda, I think. She had white white teeth

and laughed at everything I said. She seemed the perfect mate
for this new world I'd been born into that night after hitching down
from Syracuse. Ahead somewhere is the rocky driveway

down to Buzzy's college rental on the lake. Turns are the hardest times
to stay on a roof. One side of the body loses its grip, the other
wants to keep hurtling forward; but I've studied this before

at slower speeds in warmer weather with less tequila. I squint
as the engine slows, dig in my nails, wrap my left foot around the roof edge,
press down and ride the turn into the woods, reeling in my right side

and clamping it to the roof as we straighten. To cheers below, I smile
into the blackness split by the white beams of Buzzy's headlights.
I forget about the second turn and this time my left foot loses hold.

I hang for a moment like a flag, my legs spread wide grasping the air,
my right hand flailing at the night. A month from graduation,
life stretches ahead in incremental bits. I want to both freeze it

and skip ahead to the good parts. As my fingernails scrape
across the roof and I finally launch into the night,
my only thought is *shit, shit, shit, shit, shit.*

I fly between the pines lining the hill down to Lake Cayuga,
snapping off their brittle branches. Above the high-pitched whine
of wind, brakes screech and stones skitter in the driveway.

When I hit, I roll twice and land with an ooomph
against a smooth pine trunk. Buzzy and the others
scramble through the trees, swearing as they're poked

and prodded by branches, hollering, *Jack! Jack Jack!*
I just lost my glasses, I say. The moon slides out from behind a cloud –
Or maybe it was there the whole time. *Thank you,* I whisper.

I stand, check again for wounds, dust off the pine needles
and stumble up the hill. The wind roars behind me off the long finger
of glacial lake formed two million years ago and named for an Iroquois tribe

long exiled to Canada. And I realize, if there is a god of stupidity
he's not a vengeful god. He is trying to save us, but there is just
too much stupidity in the world to save every one, every time.

The Poetry Teacher

In the great poetry factories of China,
I tell my students, *each poet*
must produce a poem every ten minutes.

Students hunch over blue-lined papers.
They clutch pens like wild quills.

Randall Jarrell, I say, *said poets*
stand in thunderstorms
hoping to get hit
five or six times in their lives.

But the room is cold, say the students
and the water colder.

We are seeding the clouds, I say.
We are speeding the clashing fronts.
We are standing to our hips in water.

They scribble like buoys caught in a headwind.

Our factory is a ship, I say,
hunting for storms in the sea.
I roll marbles in each hand
to trouble their cadence.
See the lightning in the distance!

But we are sinking, say the students.

You must learn to swim, I say,
To breathe under water.

Glub glub, say the students.

The fish have little flippers, I say,
and the ocean is vast.

Water magnifies their panicked faces.

Don't flail your arms, I say,
but they can't hear me.

White paper rectangles rise, furl, unfurl.
Pens sink like harpoons into the deep.

I squint against the shock of lightning
illuminating skeletons of mackerel,
floundering against the black sea.

After the Funeral

I emptied his bookshelves
into cardboard liquor boxes
drove them to the library
for their end of summer sale
box after box
carried from the car
to a giant trailer
in the back lot
imagining buyers
fingering the titles
running a nail
along a line of text
lips moving in a whisper
the spines cracked like hymnals

Holy Shitballs!

The radio's off so the kids can sleep.
In back, their faces smush
into my mother-in-law's shoulders,

their breath slow and muffled.
The tires da-thump da-thump on the road.
Our high beams split the night

and pull us home. Joan's probably nodding
between them, repeating her prayers for Harmony
as if she'd willed this happy, tired

Thanksgiving night drive.
Anne's head slides to rest on her window.
Our breathing synchronizes to sighs

and silence — when Zak shouts *Holy Shitballs!*
Joan gasps. Anne sticks a sharp fingernail in my thigh
in case I'd forgotten I had insisted *Ace Ventura*

was fine for a five year old, ignoring her insistence
that I listen to the ratings. The ratings!
I picture my twelve-year-old self, red-faced,

hands gesturing wildly and my father shrugging,
stuttering, "You're just not ready."
And now Anne's found a website

that counts the shits and fucks
and breasts and butts. But I get it.
He's five. I know the sharp pain

of parenthood without her fingernail reminder.
I'm supposed to save him from moments like this,
when the joy of *Holy Shitballs!* wears off

and in the silent aftermath he begins
to realize what he's done, imagines
his grandmother reciting prayers for him.

But that *Holy Shitballs!* was such joy. Some sounds
light up the brain's pleasure zones,
want to be felt in the mouth, heard in open air

echoing in your own little voice – like the *Shit Howdy!*
I'd heard exclaimed in happy surprise by the pseudo cowboys
I knew in Colorado, or my friend Guy's *Fuckin' A* shouts

of frustration. How can you count and measure that?
In the dark silence of the car, I feel relief.
At least I didn't take Erin, who sighs now peacefully,

still innocent of the joy of swearing
as Joan prays for our souls or perhaps
muffles her laughter and Zak wonders how

the echo of *Holy Shitballs* could turn so quickly
to the I-never-should-have regret
that often follows great joy – the realization

that you can't go backwards. No one speaks.
The tires keep their beat in the cold night.
We each nurse our own thoughts in the warm car. Until

in the darkness Erin whispers, *Ho-ly Shit-balls,*
slow and careful as if memorizing a prayer,
then seems to fall back to sleep.

Smokin' A Real Cool Brand

I

In 1964, my sister and her ninth grade friends smoked in our basement.
I was in fourth grade and they were like grown women to me
with breasts and mascara and so damn confident. I'd let them brush my hair,
paint my nails, anything to stay in that circle of warm hands and cool chatter.
"Look! He doesn't cough," Chrissy'd say and hand me a Marlboro.

And I'd inhale, hold it in, and play my part as my lungs tightened,
smoke scraping my throat, my head reeling from euphoria
and lack of oxygen, my eyes watering, but I was not going to cough
until I'd blow it out, swallow hard and shrug. "Yeah, been smoking for years."

II

I was 13 when my grandmother got caught giving me cigarettes,
sharing her Salems that I smoked with Andy Dolph in the woods
behind his house. My parents were pissed. "How could you?" my mother asked,
but Nanny only cried. I kept saying, "It's my fault," but no one listened.
My mother began to cry. My father got quiet and still.

Outside the dogwoods sprouted little white blossoms.
The pale afternoon sky slid to evening. I was grounded for two weeks
and sent to fume in my room. Where did all that anger come from?
I once dreamed of saying, "Bond... James Bond"
before pulling a smoke out of my silver cigarette case.

III

But by seventh grade I was all Cool Hand Luke, taking a drag and saying,
"Sometimes nothin' can be a real cool hand." In 1967, 40% of adults smoked.
I could buy a pack of Lucky Strikes for 35 cents from the machine
in the back of the Chinese restaurant across from St. Catherine's.

JFK smoked. LBJ smoked. The Beatles smoked.
The Pope smoked. Well, maybe not the Pope, but every teen
wanted to be James Dean and every girl wanted to be Audrey Hepburn
waving her cigarette as she flirted in *Breakfast at Tiffany's*.

IV

And what a great way to meet girls, moving from "You want a smoke?"
to "Want a drag?" to sometimes when the clouds aligned, sharing a puff.
No shit! I sat in my room dreaming of Megan Slater and how
she was probably sitting at the Wall smoking with Tommy Murphy.

How when she tried to teach me to blow smoke rings,
her puckered lips wrapped around a Marlboro, forming an O of red
to launch circles of smoke so perfect I poked a finger through them
and pretended to hand them back. She gave me the butt and I inhaled,
watched the head ignite and blew thin wobbly ovals that wavered,
collapsed and vanished into the breeze behind Riverside School.

Megan's blue eyes squinted, she laughed, took a drag, leaned in,
pressed her open lips into mine and blew into my mouth.
My throat opened, my chest rose, my fingers reached for the blond curls
on the back of her neck and she taught me to kiss like teaching me to dance.
If it wasn't love, it was as close as I'd ever been.

V

It all started with a Marlboro – out of a red and white box
we'd tap three times to pack tight before opening, tall black letters
a red and gold crest framed by two thoroughbreds on hind legs,
the gold strip pulled with a flick to unwrap the cellophane.

I sat in my room and steamed, dreamed of being older,
of smoking in the living room, flicking my ashes into Dad's ashtray
with the St. Michael's seal – right next to his own gray clump of pipe tobacco,
or driving a Mustang with the top down, lit Marlboro dangling from my lips
as I squint one eye and nod to the girls hanging out on Sound Beach Avenue.
It was spring for god's sake! I couldn't just sit there and watch my life go by.

VI

On the second Saturday of my grounding, I snuck out at 2:00 am
to meet Megan and Dave Oldham and Maura Dolan at the swings
behind the elementary school and we played drop the ash,

and kissed and told each other secrets. I snuck back in
as the birds stirred and the light shifted from purple to a pale blue
and my dad snorted and rolled onto his back.

Later I hunched into the open bathroom window
and inhaled and dreamed of Megan's lips. The smoke rose from lungs
to eyes to brain like warm water filling a beaker. My head grew light
and I sighed, exhaled through the screen and repeated until I squeezed
the last rush out of the speckled filter and flushed, sprayed the air
and washed my hands and was shocked when I came downstairs
and my mother told me to stop smoking in the bathroom.

VII

It wasn't just about women. It was Bob Dylan and the Marlboro Man
and Mick Jagger and Frank Sinatra. By ninth grade, I was already saying,
"Quittin's easy. I've done it hundreds of times." But who wanted to quit?
How else to spice up a dull day if I wasn't meeting Mickey Jagozinsky,
the wildest kid in Eastern Junior High, in the second floor bathroom
and standing on the toilet and blowing smoke out the window?

Smoking became a ritual, how I made new friends, moved girl friend
to girlfriend, and announced to the world I wasn't some doofus
afraid of his dad's shadow. I had my daily rites – that first cigarette
that woke my brain, that post school cigarette that said I was free,

that post dinner cigarette that settled my stomach, that before bed cigarette
that told my body, "Relax, close your eyes and dream."
Quitting was like leaving a cult: the lonely nights, the smoker friends
reeling you back in with a wink or a pack left behind in my car.
Or losing a lover: the aches, the doubts, the dizziness, the old haunts avoided.

VIII

I quit for a year in high school when I couldn't run a mile without wheezing
and coughing up brown phlegm, and for six months in college
because we bet the rent; but I always slid back – mooching Camels in bars
to chase my chaser, bumming smokes at rest stops to kill time while driving,
sharing smokes in discos with girls I hoped would take me home.

Quitting meant quitting Megan, and Nanny, who after we got caught said,
"I can't give you cigarettes," pointed to the drawer in her dresser,
and added, "But you know where they are." And Chrissy's sexy friends
in the basement. And Nicky. If I wasn't a smoker, who was I?

IX

It took a gun to make me stop, a shotgun blast
when I wandered too far forward and a quail flushed sideways,
followed out of the dense vines by a spray of birdshot from Dan's gun,
spinning me to one knee thinking I'd shot my own gun
and it had recoiled into my ribs. I peeled up my sweatshirt

to see forty red pellet wounds, threw up later when I tried to smoke,
pissed blood. X-Rays showed a constellation of white pellets across my chest
and my CAT scan was a storyboard of bright BBs in my liver and kidney
and elbow and ribs. By the time I was out, I hadn't smoked in two weeks.

And those red drops of blood leaking out of my gut had done their job,
along with the PSAs of blackened lungs and Nanny's boyfriend Zeke
inhaling through the hole where his larynx used to be.

X

When the smoke cleared, the gunshot washed away all the anger,
the wishing for a different life, the pushing against my parents,
the balancing on the razor's edge of adrenaline and stupidity
– all was gone. Leaving an acute awareness of my good fortune.

Still, on a fall day, when smoke wafts from some rebel's cigarette,
I follow it, inhaling, closing my eyes, feeling the sweet lightness in my brain
and it all comes back: Megan's kiss, the pride in Chrissy's eyes,
the Boy's Room door opening and Mr. Loughran calling, "Who's in there?"

Writing Your Own Obituary

A neighbor fell out his window Monday morning.
The paper says he was a family man, excelled at crosswords,
hoped to finish hiking the Appalachian Trail this fall.
His life shrunk to a paragraph in the back of the paper.
I'm eating oatmeal and almonds, reading the obits

while Anne catches up with the Kardashians,
fast forwarding through commercials.
She thinks I'm wrong insisting the Kardashian brother
is putting on weight for the ratings. "They've seen
the numbers for *Biggest Loser* and *Dance Your Ass Off.*"

"I feel sorry for him," she says. "They just pick on him."
"It's reality TV!" I say. "He can choose his troubles.
Hire Body by Jake. Be known as the guy who lost weight."
I study the smiling faces of the dead, the names
(Arnold, Alexa, Bonazzo), ages (54, 86, 25!), try

to tease out causes (died suddenly, a courageous battle,
entered eternal rest). When Alfred Nobel
read his obit headline, *The Merchant of Death is Dead*,
after a paper confused him with his brother,
he decided to be known for peace instead of dynamite.

We regular Joes don't get headlines – just name
and narrow paragraph. In Aunt Teresa's Ireland
you were known by your troubles – "Is that the Donnellys
with the drowned boy?" she'd ask. "Or the Donnellys
with the mother kicked by the mule?" – final acts cling

like headlines to their kin. When I was shot
while hunting quail, the local headline read,
Man Shoots Friend, Not Bird, rather than *Teacher Dead*

at 29, but when the blast first swung me around, when
I dropped to one knee and raised my shirt

to see forty bloody pellet holes in my ribs,
when I later peed blood, I thought, "Get married,
have children, live a life worth summarizing
in a newspaper paragraph." Writing your own obit
is an eighth grade assignment: *President Powers*

Dead at 86, a New Age grab for all you desire:
Million Dollar Poet Buys the Farm. Write it
ten times a day and it will come true. But
I know the right answer: three children raised,
crosswords solved, hopes to hike some trail

some day, outline a life well lived. No amount
of headline pun will dress up *Bill Payer Perishes*,
Kept Lawn Trim and Green,
Kids Stayed (Mostly) Out of Trouble.
"Is there another Kardashian brother?" I ask Anne.

"One who opted out – teaches special ed in Ventura,
drives a Camry?" But she's clicked off the set
and we stare at the sudden blackness of the screen.
Outside, basketballs echo off the pavement.
Neighborhood dogs bark greetings and gossip.

Family Vacation 1965

In Providence, they put Nanny between us to stop the punch wars
        I was losing to Donny, though I would never admit it until my bruised
and battered biceps fell off my shoulder; even then I wouldn't cry,

wouldn't give Donny the satisfaction of knowing he'd won,
        wouldn't give my parents an excuse to move me into the way-back
where Ellen read surrounded by luggage, or between them

in front where Chrissy bobbed her head like some dashboard Virgin Mary,
        smiling like she never did anything wrong — which isn't true
since that's why she was sitting there in the first place.

Now I felt sorry for Nanny on her first vacation to the Cape trapped
        between bored ten-year-old me and more bored thirteen-year-old Donny;
we could only stare out the window for so long before the monotony

drove us to team up and start watching her lips, saying what she said
        at the same time she said it, until she begged, *Please boys, stop.*
It's not funny, as we begged along until my father swung his arm over the seat

and threatened, *Don't make me pull over*, slapping blindly with his hand
        as my mother pleaded, *Please Don, watch the road*, and the car
swung back and forth in traffic like a dog straining against a leash.

Then Dad slammed on his brakes and swerved into the line
        for the Cape exit, and we all panted in relief and excitement
as if returning from our wild selves, glad to have survived again

until at the Bourne Bridge, cars backed up at the circle,
        their roofs piled high with coolers, bikes and beach chairs,
Donny asked if I wanted to see who could hit the softest—

and I reached across Nanny and brushed his biceps
        and he reached across and clocked me, knuckle twisting
to reach the bone, and as I cried out, he smiled and said, *You win.*

Two Weeks After Judgment Day

The first time I ate mangos in a taco in some funky Nantucket restaurant,
I kept saying, *What are these?* and Anne kept saying, *Mangos! Where
have you been?* Where have I been? How could I have missed mangos?

Why didn't I tell Alice, *Yes, of course. You'll be fine?* And why don't I call
my mother? On Sunday she was afraid – her voice little and confused.
They don't want me to go. Everyone's turned against me. Who? Why?

She couldn't say. And playing in the back of my head all week is Steely Dan:
*Are you with me Dr. Wu? Dah ta dah dah shadows ... Are you crazy?
Are you high? Or just an ordinary guy who has done all he can do?*

It's two weeks after Judgment Day and everyone is accounted for.
No one I know has risen. A small part of me is disappointed –
the part that loves math for the right answers, that wants things resolved

one way or the other. Alice got bad news today about her heart.
She wouldn't go into details but a pacemaker won't do and surgery is planned.
It'll be fine, she says, but I know she's just reassuring herself.

Meanwhile I mow the lawn, take Charlie for a walk, fill the car with gas
and eat blueberry mango pancakes for dinner. Maybe I have it wrong
and the judging and the ascending are two different days

– confused by those ornate medieval paintings of white-soled virgins
rising into purple sky, their feet dangling in the ether, robes pulled tight
against cold winds. Below naked sinners writhe and rue their sensual lives.

Just in case, my mother used to say, *Just in case you're wrong.*
And I still wonder – I'd ask if she'd tell me – if she secretly baptized my children
in a citizen's baptism out of a cup of juice or a toilet bowl so they wouldn't suffer

if their parents were wrong. When my nephew Matt was eleven he announced
there was no Santa Claus. While we covered the ears of his young cousins,
he strutted the righteous strut – the man of the house, messenger of truth

– until Christmas Eve. *I do believe*, he said, figuring that if he didn't,
Santa wouldn't believe in him. So he recanted – just in case.
And those poor believers who poured all their savings into billboards

to spread the word? Probably high – like lottery ticket buyers – on possibility,
the brain pleasure zones lighting up CAT scans on dreams of winning.
But who am I to judge? Little miracles light up my cortex closer to home.

Head down to the dark soil, I dream of the tart surprise of mango, of pale feet
dangling from purple clouds, of eleven-year-old Matt crying *I do believe! I do!*

Man on the Floor

I was thirteen walking through my sister's dorm as the coeds yelled,
    "Man on the floor!
Man on the floor!" and I, not yet a man but hoping, stood in that hallway soaking
    in that mix
of annoyance and flirtation. My idea of a woman then was Courtney Carron

and I dreamed of getting a hand under her tight shirt. My idea of a man
    was my father's
pay-check-earning, pipe-smoking, golf-ball-whacking, bourbon-swilling silence
    or James Bond's
unstirred cool. Once, my dad, after an afternoon of golf and a cart

of cold beers, broke a rib when the mower overheated and kicked back
    into his chest.
I'd heard the mower roar and stop, roar and stop, watched my father
    search through the grass
before screwing something back in and jerking the cord again,

but I didn't know until later the mower was out of oil. So when my father tiptoed
    around the house,
saying, "I'm fine," through gritted teeth, I wanted to shout, "Just say it hurts" and
    "Just say
you're an idiot." Of all the things I'd sworn I'd do differently,

my ability to admit my idiocy has never developed. I've learned to apologize, but –
    there's always a "but"
as I explain why every stupid thing I've ever done seemed like a good idea
    at the time, and I wonder
if the girls were really yelling, "Idiot on the floor! Idiot on the floor!"

The first year I taught, I wore sneakers to school because I didn't have adult shoes.
    My boss told me to take charge:
use a point system, assign seats and buy wingtips. But the class already seemed so

oppressive.
I threw her a bone and got semi-comfortable shoes that weren't too dorky.

Those shoes seemed like one more part of the disguise I was sure they'd all
     figure out someday.
They say the last to know they have power are those who have it. Is that true
     for the clueless as well?
The day before he died, my father woke in his hospital bed and said,

"Everything in Springfield is just like it was – Dreisen's Fountain
     McDougal's Grocery.
"Did you see anyone there?" I asked, not sure if it was dream or dementia.
     But he'd turned to the wall.
Sensing the end, hoping really, since the next stop was a nursing home

he'd made clear he never wanted – I went to get my family from the lounge.
     All I could hear was the squeak
of my semi-adult shoes on linoleum in that hospital hall. Stroke and dementia
     had softened my father,
made him kinder. "You're a better father than I was, " he said one night

after he'd watched me coach Will in some peewee basketball game, and if he
     wasn't my father
I would have hugged him. "Thanks" is all I could sputter. Some Septembers,
     the ninth grade boys' attempts
to saunter down the halls are so uncertain it looks as if the ground is shifting.

I want to shout, "Man on the floor!" to buoy their strides if only for a moment.
     I think of having yelled
at my own son, now probably back from school and rooted to the couch
     and his computer,
and I cringe at how much I sound like my own father, sarcastic, impatient.

When I open the door he's already glued to his laptop eating Chex Mix.
     "Sorry," I say.
"What?" he says, keeping one eye on the screen. "I'm an idiot," I say.
     And he flips his computer shut
and says, "What?" Before I can say, "But..." the dog starts barking.

His tail sweeps magazines off the table. The dog picks up a toy and begins
     a whine that sounds like he's singing.
My son is asking, "What are you doing?" I shake my head. My son's brow
     furrows. But I can only lay back
on the floor, close my eyes and dream of waking up and starting all over.

II

Spittin' Image

Same thing without the pipe, the caricaturist said
in Provincetown, when I, at five, followed my father
into the chair and he sketched the same
horned-rim glasses, snub nose, wavy brown hair
brushed back in front – only child size.
My reactions ranged from flattered then
to angry at 14 to bewildered in afro
and Fu Manchu at 20, to mildly amused at 40

when I thought I'd been successful in my campaign
to be the anti-him. And now as he struggles
to decipher a hotdog shack menu and asks
the same question again and again,

I nod when the waitress says, *Must be your dad*,
and I help him onto the wobbly stool.

Counting

Whitney Houston is dead, found in a hotel bathtub
just before the Grammys
      as if she'd just slid down – awake or asleep –
      and let the waters claim her.
And the airwaves are full of *The Preacher's Wife*
and *The Body Guard*

and "I Will Always Love You" which I learned
was written by Dolly Parton –
      a fact I can't quite wrap my ear around.
      And as Anne watches the funeral
broadcast live from a grand Baptist church
in Newark, I wonder how such talent

can lead to such misery, and if the two are related
at all. I mark up some papers,
      read the baseball scores, give the cat his pill
      and wonder if celebrity
is the greatest drug of all. How else to explain
Reality Show Whitney

dragging her plump preteen daughter into our
living rooms
      as she and Bobby camp out, pretending
      to have ordinary lives. All
the has-beens and almost-weres on *Celebrity Rehab*
try to reclaim their lives

or die famous; and think how season four ended
with the mother
      of an over-dosed rock star forgiving
      his drug-addicted rock-star buddy

who watched him die. She said, "You don't have
to live a fantastic, incredible

celebrity life. You can live a boring predictable life.
And you cannot believe
        how rich that is, until you're in it." And though
        I don't believe, I understand
religion's pull to give certainty and dignity
to ordinary life. I understand

celebrity's lure to make a memorable life in this
all-publicity's-good-publicity world.
        And that night, when Anne
        orders the Devil's Roll and I
the Mango Tango and the Godzilla Roll and eat them
with the chopsticks still attached

because I'm embarrassed to ask for a fork, I watch
the two-year-old at the next table
        eat her rice and mimic everything her
        four-year-old brother does, and the baby
in a high chair two tables down smiles and gurgles
at the finely-tweezed college girls across the aisle

who flirt with him, and I wonder if this is it – the tang
of the mango with the crunch
        of spicy tuna, the wide-cheek-boned smile
        of the waitress whose name
I can never remember, the hot tea, the soy sauce
I dip my rolls in,

the crowd in the restaurant that ignores us so we can
eavesdrop and catch snippets
        of their lives in quick glances. In a dream last
        night I sat across
from a white-haired woman with pearls
and startling blue eyes talking about "the magic

of cities," how they were "invented by the Puritans
in New England." I know she's someone,
        but I don't know who. And though I know
        what she says isn't true, I am infatuated

with her certainty. Even after I wake, I can still see
the textured red of lipstick on her cigarette,

the smoke rising in a lazy curl, her elegant veined
hands dancing as she speaks. Who
        doesn't love a celebrity rising up with a fresh
        new story? Who doesn't shake their heads
when they fall? Who doesn't sigh and settle back
into the dull safe waters of anonymity?

I wonder if Whitney closed her eyes and slipped
beneath the water
        like a child counting to one hundred while
        the other children hide,
palms pressed to her face: *one one thousand,*
two one thousand, three one thousand, four.

How to Write a College Essay

Start with your greatest loss, biggest obstacle, the woman you loved, the man you killed. Open your heart. Relax. Show the real you. Write like your hair is smoldering. This is the most important paper of your life; be unique. Never mention the word "special." Be specific: the time your mother wished she'd never adopted you; the night your father died in the fire. Make the reader see the veins in her neck, feel the words strike, the door slam. See you in the garage smoking by the turpentine; see the garage ignite.

Breaker 1-9

Teaching Granny CB language seems cruel now.
    If she wanted the salt or even
just to ask where Mom and Dad went to dinner,

my sister Ellen or I would say, "Negatory, Good Buddy,"
    and ask for her 10-20. Or "Breaker 1-9. What's your handle?"
until finally she'd say, "Oh, Jackie. This is the Silver Granny.

Can you pass the butter?" "That's a big 10-4," we'd shout
    and slide the yellow slab her way. She'd be proud of that butter.
She'd earned it. And later that night when she fell

and gashed her shin on her walker, we had a language
    to avoid the raw details of the present while I picked her up,
stopped the bleeding and poured seltzer on the rug

to sop the stain that spread instead into a map
    of the nineteenth century Ireland she was born into –
and seemed to me still lived. "10-4, Jackie," she agreed,

balancing over me on numb feet when I pointed
    to where Dublin would be. "Where'd you live, Silver Granny?"
"In the North," she said, aiming a crooked finger below Newry

to Clenchagora. "Can't hear you, Good Buddy," I said.
    "Give me a handle at least." "Over and out," she croaked
in a dry-throated brogue, and dropped back into her chair,

and laughed. "Clench-a-gor-a," I said slowly, and "Be-ta-hush" —
    which Granny claimed was "Shut up" in Gaelic —
and "Pug-a-me-owm," which made her ears burn,

but which she wouldn't confirm meant, "Kiss my ass."
    We could hear eighteen-wheelers downshifting in the night,
 the sound echoing off the muddy Mianus River

down the hill from our house – traveling the same bridge
  that would drop a hundred-foot span onto the rocks
ten years later along with a couple of cars

and a semi or two. Across the sea the "bad 'uns,"
  as Granny called them, were still bombing one pub
for serving the British and another pub for not,

just like they were when she came through Ellis Island
  in 19 and 13. Years later, on a road trip,
I called from Colorado. "Hello!" Granny shouted,

her fear of technology making her brogue thicker.
  "Granny, this is Jack." I knew I should have hung up
after the tenth ring. "Jackie's not home!" she said.

"Granny, this is me: Jackie." As if shouting
  across a canyon, she repeated, "Jackie's not home."

Carry/Miscarry

I step into our tiny bathroom and stare at the open toilet. Swirls of red marbleize the clear water. It might be the flush of heavy period, but I know in that dark red clump in the bottom of the bowl is a little body. *Container* I say to myself, slog down the stairs, through the dining room, a deep sea diver though the foreign world we now inhabit, open the cupboard next to the stove. Out tumble Tupperware with blue lids, old potato salad containers. Which could hold our baby, still, un-born? The doctor'd said, *Bring in the fetus. We'll take a look.* Three days of waiting. This morning Anne gasped and rushed to the bathroom; I listened to the splash and knew. I choose the biggest, best Tupperware, pull a ladle out of the drawer, climb back up the stairs, glance toward Anne face-down on the bed, walk into the bathroom and kneel beside the toilet. Fishing into the bowl, I scoop up a clump of matted blood and peer at it for some vague human shape.*I'm bleeding*, Anne said Saturday, *I think it's dead.* Holding the milky container up to the window's gray November light, I search the ragged clump with the spoon for a ten-week-old em-bryo, for beginnings of fingers, toes, a tiny skull. Against the white porcelain, the red water disperses into opaque clouds. It must still be down there. I kneel again, dip the ladle deep into the water and feel myself rise up twenty feet above the room, able to look down on my still kneeling self, the faded linoleum floor, the back of my brown curly head peering down into the bowl, feeling for a tiny child not-to-be and finding it with a mixture of satisfaction and disgust. Watching both from above and through my body-eyes, I see the ladle in my hand rise slowly from the murk, the water drain off stringy clots of blood, revealing a not-yet being with thin veiny arms and legs and head, with eye lids sealed shut and my ceiling-self flies back to my kneeling-self, joining in awe and grief, wondering how it ever works, and why it sometimes doesn't, how fingers know when to grow, tiny lungs know when to open, how neurons know to reach out and grab each other, knowing I can't explain it to Anne or anyone and wondering if we'll ever have the nerve to try again.

Summer Drunk

Anne texts from Colorado tracking flights as Hurricane Irene batters Bermuda
like a vengeful drunk. My mother calls. She can't put in her new hearing aid.
"I thought this," she says, "was my left ear, but everyone says it's my right."

Over the phone, I try to explain how to put that dried alien
into her ear. Accept this: Anne will worry, my mother has learned
all she can, and summer is ending. At the end of a week, perfect

for peaches, tomatoes and hurricanes, rain begins to pelt the windows
and the trees sway like one a.m. drunks doing the dance of the barely upright.
Anne's plane has been cancelled and the kitchen lights flicker as I carve

the peach skin off in fuzzy spirals that drop into the sink,
then dice the orange pulp into a salad of red tomatoes
and pale cucumbers. The power goes out with a hmmph.

I lean over the now black sink and hold onto the image of the rosy
speckles on the pale peel curled on the porcelain. Drunk
on the moment I'm in, I close my eyes, find a fork and alternate bites

of peach and tomato, peach and tomato, peach and tomato.

Donny One Note

A lady in my Sunday morning Yoga4Everybody class holds her *Om*
      3 or 4 seconds longer
than her fellow yogis. While the rest of us are contemplating our inner
      Oms, she's still belting out hers –
her alto *mmm* vibrating the studio windows and taking me out
      of the moment

and into the memory of my father holding out the last note of every song
      at our Thanksgiving dinners
decades ago when after a few bourbons and a full plate of meat
      and potatoes, the Irish relatives
would start chirping. Uncle Johnny would request *Anchors Away*
      or Dad would launch into *My Way*

and the table joined in slurry harmony – a cacophonous chorus
      that scared the dog –
holding out the last word until they dropped one by one and it was just Don
      riding that note
while the rest of us caught our breath, sipped our coffee and swallowed
      a forkful of pecan pie.

An aunt from Long Island dubbed him Donny One Note and he wore
      that moniker like a heavyweight belt.
So I let the lady *om* away. I think – my eyes are closed, of course –
      it's the drama teacher from the local college
who can't let 30 years of diaphragm training go to waste, can't resist
      projecting her *om* to the poor yogis

in the back row. Later that day Zak – who at twenty-two has started
      pulling boxes of photos
out of the closets at my mother's retirement home and cataloging them
      and tracing the family tree on-line –

hands me a folded piece of blue-lined paper filled with a list in my father's
　　square-lettered script:

Dr. Siefert thinks I had a stroke. Tests confirm. Bills getting harder to do.
　　As if he was leaving notes
to himself like the tattooed man in *Momento* that he can find later
　　to piece together his life
and I tell Zak about Donny One Note and the cherry-handled Peterson
　　pipe Dad loved to smoke after dinner,

that I swear I smell sometimes on walks in late fall, and the red
　　leather chair he loved to settle in
to scan his minions (his books and us) and I can almost hear that
　　Waaaaaaaaaaaaaay
one long *a* held until the windows begin to hum. He climbs into the note,
　　settles into that red chair,

maybe stuffs the pipe with Bond Street Tobacco and nurses it into a burn,
　　watches the smoke curl to the ceiling,
up to the notched-wood beams he'd picked out himself, and stays
　　right there in that moment.

How to Talk to Old People

When your father's stroke loosens his tongue, ask about early memories: the soda fountain on Hungry Hill, running cross country without a coach. Ask until he stares past you like he's back in Springfield: hearing the parrots in Forest Park as he and Jack Facey outrun them all.

When your grandmother's stuck in her seat by the window, ask her "What did they call farts in Ireland, Granny?" Or say, "I'm going out with some friends to shoot heroin and steal cars." "Oh Jackie," she'll say.

When Parkinson's confines your mother to bed, her bones curled beneath the blanket, all eyelids and beak, her heart still beating somehow, ask, "Do you want to dance a salsa?" Ask, "Are the aides beating you?" Dangle questions like worms until she reacts.

When threatening to leave is the only thing that brings her alive, say, "Time to go," and her eyes will pop open – pale blue, red-rimmed. She'll search your face, the room, the air for a question before fixing on your curls, now as white as your father's and say, "You going to dye your hair?" and you'll laugh. "Should I?" "Too late," she'll say, smiling before dozing off again.

Bless Me Father

At the teen Mass, Father Tom gathered us around him on the altar
and said being Catholic is all about forgiveness, but the Catholic school kids
just smirked and poked each other with elbows. They saw a clear hierarchy

– God, the Pope, priests, nuns, them and public school Catholics like me –
that they enforced by tracking the priests at dances or nuns at open gym
and, when the coast was clear, zooming in on our weakness, enforcing order

with head locks and nuggies, shoving us into walls, crowing like baboons
or dinging our ears as we huddled in pews before Thursday confession.
The priests were busy in their little rooms and the nuns patrolled the aisles

yanking yelping sinners from the church by those same tender ears.
So when Father Tom, trying to be cool with teen Masses, served real wine,
we gulped and gulped. He filled it higher and higher until I realized

he had to drink the leftovers and told everyone to sip, leaving a full chalice
that took him three chugs to finish. But when I saw him watery-eyed
and wobbly wiping the cup clean, I waved off the Catholic school boys

slapping me on the back as if welcoming me to their club, waved off a ride
from Brian's mom to walk off the guilt and stopped at the bridge over 95,
to watch the cars whoosh, whoosh under me in a rhythm so calming

I dreamed of hitching a ride to a distant land where I could believe in forgiveness
until a gear-grinding semi downshifted, shaking the cement beneath my feet.

Being a Dick

Once when I was painting the Milligan's house,
      I walked into the kitchen with Dick Jr. to find Dick Sr.
and a grey-haired man in overalls holding an old plumber's wrench.

When the elder Dick said, "Have you met my son Dick?" the handyman smiled
      and offered a hand. "Dick Swanson," he said. And I, figuring, you know,
when in Rome, offered my own hand. "Dick Powers," I said.
      "Pleased to meet ya." The Milligans laughed, Dick the Handyman
offered a firm handshake and life went on. Except the next fall,

I got a job at the middle school and on my way to lunch was greeted
      by a smiling Handyman Dick. He taught eighth grade science
on the second floor. Each day at noon he'd smile and shout, "Hi Dick!"
      and I'd wave. "Hi, Dick!" For thirty seconds every day I was Dick.
I wondered: if I taught next door, would we hang out together?

Would I start helping out with handyman jobs on weekends?
      Would I leave teaching to form *Dick & Dick: Handyman Solutions*
or *Two Dicks: Handymen.* Let's face it: being Jack is easy,
      but being Dick? That's tough. You're crushed or grow stronger,
proud of all the Dicks who've persevered,

who exchange hearty handshakes in a secret society
      like I glimpsed in that kitchen: four Dicks sharing a laugh.

Philtrum Guards

The nose hairs of the Citgo station cashier can almost be braided,
hanging instead in matching half-inch ponytails bracketing his philtrum –
the groove that runs from lips to nose that I can only name

because it was the target for the second knuckle of a straight punch
in Tai Kwon Do. Perhaps these twin twines are guards and the man,
a priest of an ancient cult and his time here at Citgo a penance

or assignment to an outpost welcoming fellow travelers in from the cold
western world of Pick Six tickets, flavored Skoal cans and fluffy purple pens.
He counts the dollar bills and returns the neat stack to his drawer.

The hairs sway in the gentle wind of his slow Ujjayi breaths,
that ocean breath the Vinyasas practice, and perhaps I only need
to give a sign – a nickel left in the leave-a-penny-tray or a query

about those philtrum guards – to be invited in to the back room dojo
littered with ceremonial swords and meditation mats, a magically expanding
room ending in a thick oak door that opens to a glittering temple

– the first steps to rejoining my journey to higher consciousness.
I hand him two bucks for my coffee and he hands me change,
punching my frequent buyer card without a word. I return to my car,

slide the nozzle into the tank, inhale and wonder if it's the wafting
gas fumes that have me muddling all this vaguely Eastern minutiae,
thinking I've lost my way on some mystical, vaguely remembered journey.

On another day I might have just imagined him as someone who'd lost a bet,
but today as the sunset turns the February sky orange, an elderly man
in neighboring car twirls his nose hairs. I blink and he's just picking his nose.

The gas stops. I squeeze a few more pennies in to round her off at $37.50.
When I look up the old nose-picker is gone. The neighboring pumps
are manned by teenagers in shiny vans or European sedans

and a stubbly-faced guy in a dented pickup. He could be an assassin
or a house painter. I slide back into the cocoon of my car and give her a crank.
Turning down the radio, I pull up to the station window,

peer through the posters of milk sales and coffee specials,
but the glare blocks my view. As I lean across the passenger seat,
I can make out the outline of The Philtrum Guard

making change behind the counter, but then the clouds shift
and all I see is a reflection of my own scrunched up nose,
my eyes squinting at something just out of sight.

Granny's Yellow Plastic Radio

My grandmother kept a yellow plastic radio on her kitchen counter. Aerodynamic with rounded corners and plastic vents, the radio looked like it could be launched into space. The bright red dial was always tuned to the all news station. Granny wore large print dresses and her long, dark hair in a bun and always seemed to be washing pots and pans or boiling chicken. On top, a wide swath of white hair marked a stroke she had before I knew her. The only other remnant was her stiff walk as she gripped the counter, balancing on her numb feet as if on stilts. The radio broadcast the news and the weather, the news and the weather - fast paced and loud, in contrast to her slow steps. Through the window over the sink, the backyard dropped to a field of cows and a farm. Granny never looked up from scouring her pans. The announcer told of the Russians' latest evil or some terrible plane crash – interrupted by fast paced music, grabbing our attention for the latest story, just in. After Granny moved in with us, that radio sat in a basement corner covered with dust among the tables and lamps we saved after Grandpa died. Years later, when Granny lay in a nursing home waiting to die, unreceptive to the world, I searched for that radio. But the basement corner was empty, cleaned out in some mad spring cleaning. Instead, I sat next to her and described it. Turning the radio dial in my mind, I wondered what news it would be broadcasting now. But her eyes gave no flicker of recognition. She stared into space. I filled that space with a yellow plastic radio on a black Formica counter. Over a sink full of pots and pans, a window looked out over a field of cows and in the distance a big red barn and an old white farmhouse. I painted a picture of a little boy sitting on a spotless linoleum floor watching his grandmother pull her suds-covered hand out of the hot water. The radio spoke of Kennedy and Khrushchev, John Glenn and Sputnik, Mickey Mantle and fallout shelters. I avoided Granny's expressionless face, lest the picture crumble. By her slow measured breathing, I knew she'd fallen asleep. In the silence, I gazed one last time out the window at the green fields, and the black and white cows. I squeezed Granny's hand and said goodbye. I reached over her sleeping form, turned off the radio and tiptoed out the door.

On Purpose

"It was no accident," Lillian said. "I drove into that tree on purpose."
We stood in the hallway outside Miss Rafel's class. Other students passed by
gabbing, clutching books to their chests, rushing to seventh period.

Lillian's nose was broken; a ragged shoreline of yellow edged the purple
around her eyes. Her jaw was wired shut so I had to lean close to hear.
"You always seem so happy," she whispered. "Why do you want to live?"

I'd just learned for sure her name was Lillian during the week
she was in the hospital. She'd sat behind me all semester,
laughed at my jokes, complimented the drawings I did of classmates

while Miss Rafel launched into her Thoreau soliloquys. Lillian was shy, blonde,
blue eyed, all bony angles. "I don't know," I said. "Because . . . I do?"
I shrugged. She squeezed past me, mumbling, "I'm sorry. It's not a fair qu–"

"No, no," I said, turning to walk with her. "It's a great question."
I searched for a line that could save her as we walked down the dark hall,
out the door, into the first brittle sunny day of March. "Can I think about it?"

We rode bikes that day to the reservoir. I had no idea how to answer
so I brought her to Miss Jank's art class to paint watercolors of pears,
to the beach to collect horseshoe crabs on a rocky point,

to read her "Hands," my favorite story at the time, repeating the end together
again and again like a prayer. She went along with anything I proposed.
But she was sad-eyed – a muted version of her pre-crash self.

Maybe she wanted me to sweep her into my arms, but I knew that
wouldn't end well. After a week, she said, "Thanks. I think I get it,"
but never told me what she got. We returned to being friendly classmates

in a mostly boring English class until she went to Florida for April vacation
and didn't return. No one knew why. I wanted to think she found someone
with a better answer, that she was living on a beach in a rickety cabana,

writing poetry and grilling bluefish in a sand pit. But I was sure she was dead
because I couldn't answer a simple question. And I thought of her
over the years when my best friend's brother hanged himself from a tree,

when a student died in a crash that seemed more reckless than accidental,
when some rock star ate too many pills. I never found an answer.
Good genes? Good friends? Good parenting? Good luck?

Before our thirtieth reunion, we received an email of classmates
"In memoriam" with Lillian's name on top. "Of course," I said,
putting myself on the list of those who'd failed her.

Halfway through the reunion, the ballroom door slammed opened
and Lillian stepped into the spotlight shouting, "I am alive!"
Women delighted by her resurrection swarmed around her,

launching right into "remember whens." She had friends!
I snuck up to the edge of her entourage and listened. She said she heard
she'd made the list and thought, "Why not make an entrance?"

and how she'd hitchhiked to Boca Raton for spring break and decided to stay.
When I worked my way to the front, she didn't recognize me.
"Miss Rafel's class?" she asked and scrunched her nose. "Oh, yeah!

Still drawing bored students?" "No, I'm teaching bored students now," I said,
and when she laughed, her blue eyes caught the light of the chandeliers.
We talked for a few minutes, but she never brought up our conversation

in that long ago hallway, and I started to think I'd imagined it.
My role now shrunk from almost hero to failed hero to deleted extra,
I watched her walk away across the dance floor, her now curvy body

swaying to the music, hips swiveling, light catching the blond of her hair.
She carved an island of space in the sea of bodies. Her toes flexed, unflexed
as if kneading sand. Then dancers surged around her and she was gone.

Do Not Resuscitate

My dentist says when he hits 80 he'll pile on overcoats
and shovel like crazy at the first big snow.
He wants a jogging t-shirt that says, "Do Not Resuscitate!"
My sister-in-law saves the remnants of every prescription.
Her chemist husband insists they'll still be good.
I'm afraid I'd forget where I put them.
                                        After visiting my mother
I beg my wife, "Put a pillow over my face if I get like that."
Anne says they'd arrest her. My daughter says,
"Don't say that." She believes words said in jest
will come back to haunt you. "I'm not kidding," I say.
My boys just laugh.
                            In a Sunday *Times* story,
a life-long advocate of dying with dignity now nurses
her quadriplegic husband. A passing Samaritan
kept him alive after a bike crash, unaware of his wishes.
"It's so hard," his wife says. What he wants changes
from day to day and she's afraid of getting it wrong.
And like Anne, she doesn't want to be left alone.
The elderly always score highest on happiness polls,
but maybe just those who can still answer the phone.
                                                Yesterday
I watched an 80-something woman take baby steps
across the waiting room of the walk-in clinic
and wondered how she got here. As my son told the nurse
about his poison ivy, the woman shuffled across the room
each foot placed and tested before settling and moving the other.
Dressed in her Sunday best, pancake and rouge expertly applied,
she had bandages on both shins, blood leaking through
her stockings like Granny's at the end when a change
of the wind's direction could slice her skin, rice paper thin,

and open the bloodgates. "He's so tall," the woman said
when she finally sat. Her smile tentative, sincere.
"Enjoy it," she said, "They grow up so fast."

Rob Smuniewski Is Dead

Dead at 18. Hit by an 84-year-old driving a 20-year-old Honda.
Rob Smuniewski, whose engine revved higher than anyone's.
Dead. Who wrote "I love redheads" on his desk, on his locker,

who stood on a table in the cafeteria and asked a redhead to the prom,
who jumped down and danced from the room shaking his head
when she said no, who wrote a love poem to redheads
from a list of favorite words (ginger, auburn, strawberry,
freakin' and one I said he couldn't use in school) which ended
"the only way to tell if the drapes match the rug is to see the –
and that's the word you said I can't use!" Who loved his quad,

broken down on that January night. Rob Smuniewski,
who must have flown in the air like the deer I hit
last winter in Maine, shot out of the darkness, eyes as wide as mine,

both helpless to stop the sudden collision. Rob, who danced
more than walked, dead. Rob, who called the ladies "Dawl"
and the men "Coach," always neat in khakis, oxford shirts –
argyle vests and ties for game days – who told his sister,
"I don't go to school to learn; I go to entertain."
Who taught me never to ask, "Any questions?" in class
when he said, "Yeah. I have two. How come my nose

always gets sunburned first no matter what I do.
Look! I look like freakin' Rudolph! And another thing!
When you wear a robe around the house you're supposed to feel manly.

I feel like a woman. What's with that?"
Rob freakin' Smuniewski: dead. Who you knew,
even when you wanted to strangle him, couldn't find
his own off switch any more than you could,

who would later apologize and say, "You the man, Coach."
Who, when he launched into the frosty air, might have waved
to the fear-stricken driver, might have thought this will make a great story,

might have thought — as I did when my girlfriend Cam rolled her old Volvo
thirty years ago in Vermont, as the black pavement rose
to meet my passenger window — "So this is how it freakin' ends."

III

He Couldn't Remember

why he got up,
why he'd come upstairs, tapped his pockets
for a pipe he'd quit years before. No urge
to pee. No wet pants. No growling stomach.
He wandered around the bedroom, raised
the accordion blinds on the narrow window,
wondered if he'd just forgotten how bad
his memory had always been. But then it never
mattered what he'd been looking for anyway,
it's what he'd found. Like this paisley-moted
shaft of afternoon light bending
through the dusty panes; a yellow spotlight
like one from that thirties painter famous
for lonely men in a night-lit diner.
He'd seen it once in a high-ceilinged museum
while standing hand-in-hand with a black-haired,
soft-faced beauty who might once have been his wife.

Signs

I.

A friend emails a joke:

> *Jethro drives in a sweat. He has an important meeting*
> *and can't find a parking space. Looking up to heaven,*
> *he says: "Lord, take pity. If you find me a parking place*
> *I will go to Mass every Sunday and give up the reefer."*
> *Miraculously, a space appears. Jethro looks up again:*
> *"Never mind," he says. "I found one."*

"I think I'm a lot like Jethro," she writes.

II.

She hadn't emailed in months except for apologies:
Sorry I missed your birthday. I'll send a present soon.
And then: *I have breast cancer. Surgery. Chemo.*
Depression. Didn't Anne survive this? We email back.
My wife, five years from chemo, leads. I follow:
cheer the clean lymph nodes, praise medicine's progress.

Two weeks later her gift arrives: a framed page
from her wedding-present/recipe-book from friends –
a picture of a tuxedoed, Brill-Creamed, bleary-eyed,
G-and-T-toting, thirty-years-ago me under the title
Stewed Jack. Below a recipe asks for ice, gin, tonic, bitters
and me. *Insults 12 to 15*, read the serving directions.
Remember those days? Jeannie writes.

How did we survive them? I write back. Post-college/
pre-family nights spent idling, marinating in alcohol
and whatever else, ever-vigilant for fun – wasted days.

III.

Anne hides the picture from our children. I
take the dog for a walk. Cancer makes you notice things:
the still-turning-trees, crumbled walls, rows
of shuttered colonials. My old retriever strains
against the leash, sniffs each sewer drain and tree root.
I hear birds ahead, grackles, hundreds of them,
resting on their October trip south.

Their anarchy chorus dials up to max. Kelly's ears perk up
as we near the rising din. Neither of us can see them,
but we know they're there - small and black, dotting a yard
or a tree: a separate and connected mesh waiting to rise
into a rippling V. We hold tight the rise of waiting in our chests
— step-by-step across browning yards. The heat
of our working bodies fends off the breeze – holding, holding

until in a random moment the grackles rise, a swarming fabric
of black-speckled clamor from yards to trees to blue sky.

In an instant they are gone.

Chest Wounds

I wasn't horny enough for my eighth grade girlfriend.
She was older and fed me shots of vodka to get me in the mood.
I didn't like being rushed. She didn't like waiting.

I just threw up and passed out and sometimes
woke up drunk the next day. My mother was worried
about me seeing a ninth grader – pestering my brother,

complete strangers, even my knee doctor
to talk some sense into me. "Tell him he's too young," she'd say.
The doctor mumbled, "Listen to your mother," shrugged

and said something about leg lifts. I was tired of the spin-
the-bottle, over-the-bra-feel girlfriends my own age.
I was skinny, but tall and looked older than I was.

She was thrilling and scary and sometimes I hated her.
Maybe I was afraid I'd disappear. So I dug in
countering unstoppable with immovable.

But when we went to her house one Tuesday afternoon
and found her mother passed out in vomit on the living room rug,
we cleaned her up and carried her to her bed.

I wanted somehow to close that wound
as we made out in her room and began to work our way around
the bases. Maybe she thought I could pin her down

and blast her into a new life. On the bus one day,
she found a poem I wrote in English class and read it aloud.
It was about birds or fish or communism and I just wrote it

to get Mr. Zaboray to leave me alone. Her friends shrieked with laughter.
The next day at lunch I didn't sit at our table, returning instead
to my eighth grade friends. She came over, scrunched her lips.

"I don't know what you're trying to prove –" she said,
but I interrupted her. "I need to break up," I said.
She turned and walked away. "I'm sorry," I whispered,

but she wasn't listening. Her dark figure blurred, disappearing
into the shrill yellow light of the lunch room windows.

The Body

"Do you want to see the body?" my brother, Donny, asks.
      I stand in the Bijou lobby, cell phone to ear.
When I hesitate, he adds, "We could hold off
      calling Gallagher's." An hour before
I'd sat by her bed listening to her rasping,
      the hospice nurse saying, "Twenty-four hours,
maybe," her palm caressing my mother's cheek.
      I thought I had time. "No. Call them," I say.

After Dad died, I took her to the movies every Sunday.
      Better than methadone, movies made the pain
in her back disappear. She'd sit expressionless,
      floating out of her body to watch a boy train a dragon
or Owen Wilson wander through Paris. Once I took her
      to *Biutiful* and she didn't complain until the next week.
"It was okay," she said after watching *Despicable Me*.
      "At least it washed the blood out of my brain."

When I arrive, Donny and Chrissy stand around the bed.
      Ellen is stuck in Jersey. My mother's lips are warm,
but I can feel the cold seeping in. Her nose seems sharper,
      skin yellower; the stillness is shocking.
For two years she's been just a body – moved from bed
      to couch and TV by the Caribbean women who clothe her,
feed her, sit beside her reading Bibles like missionaries.
      Occasionally she'd startle us with a word or two.

Just before Dad died, they checked her into a room
      down the hall from his. After years of his dementia,
helping him dress, answering his same questions over and over,
      sleeping lightly, afraid he'd wake and wander off,
she was too tired to fight. Worn to the depths of her organs,

to her smallest spark, she never bounced back.
His mind departed while his body remained intact,
    but her mind and body left hand in hand.

On the wall above her bed hangs the pine crucifix
    that's been nailed above her sleeping head in every house
we'd ever lived in. At ten, I'd discovered a secret compartment
    with candles, cotton, a bottle of holy water and tattered paper.
I'd never told anyone until Father Hopkins came yesterday.
    "It's for last rites," he said, taking it from the wall,
sliding it open, pulling out the yellow candles, the now-dry bottle,
    the brittle paper of "Sick Call" instructions.

I don't believe, but sometimes, as I watched her disappear,
    her body and brain in cobwebs, I wished for more.
Long past talking or walking, she fed herself,
    fork rising like a rickety crane the old operator
ratcheted up by memory. When she could no longer
    go to the movies, I'd bring her chocolate.
(Her last words to me were "Hershey's Bar" when the Baby Ruths
    were rejected. A minute later she added, "With nuts.")

After she couldn't feed herself, her hand would still rise on its own
    and hover. Then drop back to her lap. After they wrap the body
and roll it out to the hearse, we divvy up the jobs: Ellen and Chris
    make phone calls. Donny handles the funeral home.
I write the obituary and eulogy. I search old albums for an obit pic
    and find her kneeling in our snowy driveway laughing
with my kids, Zak and Erin, then five and three, in snow suits;
    in another she's loading a carload of Girl Scouts into a convertible;

and, in the one I choose, at Donny's wedding, in pearls
    and elegant cotton dress, her hair coifed,
her pale blue eyes are looking at mine. I crop the photo
    to frame her face. When they take away the body,
we stare at the empty bed. The feeling of remove,
    of watching a film sets in. Donny points to the window.
"When she died," he says, "Edna opened it to release her spirit."
    I press my face into the glass and squint into the night.

Bishop Pike's Undershorts

Maggie's telling us at lunch how her 88-year-old mother kept insisting a picture
of some cousin was her own long dead brother and how Maggie'd set her straight
but her mother kept insisting. "Maggie," I said, "Can't you just give it to her?"

And rubbing it in, I told a story about my mother, who, one Christmas
near the end, thought I was my father, squeezing my hand,
laughing at some shared Springfield memory and I played along

since it was the most she'd said all day. But what I didn't tell Maggie
was how I'd had decades of preparation living elbow to elbow
as a know-it-all teen with two grandmothers killing time in my living room.

I can't remember who moved in first: Granny after Grandpa died or Nanny
after her second heart attack, but by the summer of 1966, they'd taken over
Ellen's room and the eight of us were sharing one bathroom at 21 Oval Avenue.

They called each other Mrs. Loughran and Mrs. Powers, perhaps a nod to the gap
between Granny's pagan Irish Catholic childhood – one of ten kids
in a three-room hovel, sent off at 13 to be a live-in maid – and Nanny's

New England factory working family and rumored Twenties as a flapper.
During the day they'd work through the newspaper together, sharing articles
garbled by Granny's habit of reading through the "continued on page 12's"

and into the article below. Nanny'd nod, say "Hmmm," maybe ask a question,
but mostly concentrate on pumping nicotine through her last working ventricle.
Usually I just laughed in the next room, killing my own time with a book,

picturing the two nodding heads in agreement: Granny, ever make-up free,
in gray bun, and floral tent dresses, and Nanny with dyed blonde hair, pearls
and red-lipstick-stained Salems. But one day, when Granny said,

"They found that Bishop Pike's body – wandering the desert in his underwear,"
something snapped. I needed to set things right. He was dead for Christ's sake!
You can't have the last picture of him be in his Fruit of the Looms!

I stomped in, all indignant twelve-year-old, grabbed the paper, scanned the article,
summarizing the highlights as I read: "Former Bishop of California... tracing
the steps of Jesus... Judean desert... car stuck... Listen!" I read aloud,

"'Police said he'd left clues in his wake: a map... his undershorts... glasses
– to indicate the path he'd taken. Hah!" Their surprised faces looked unconvinced.
"He wasn't wandering in his underwear!" They stared. It wasn't dual dementia –

more like I was raining on their parade. Granny said, "Oh, Jackie," Nanny added,
"You look just like your father when you're mad." Outside a dog barked,
the sun hung in the afternoon sky, some neighborhood kids played kick the can.

I can't say I thought *Just give it to them* in that moment, but the seed was planted.
I mean, would Bishop Pike really care? I dropped the paper in Granny's lap,
and took the stairs two at a time. In my wake, I heard Granny turn the page.

In Fear of Heart Attacks

Especially the big ones, the lights-out, no-time-to-negotiate
kaboomers. You can bargain with the little ones, beg
for another day, week, year. In the end, I'll ask for an extension
to see some as-yet unborn grandson's fifth grade recital.
Just wheel me in to see him in gold-buttoned blazer
and red tie, I'll be saying, Then you can take me, Lord –
I don't believe, but I like a name when I haggle.
One more trip to see Derain's London Bridge. Wheel me
one last time onto Bermuda sand. One more chance
to watch the weaving mass under the stars at Grand Central.
Then I'll go without a fight.
                                        Sure I will. I'll lie like it's bedtime
and I'm four. You think I'll know when to go? You think
I'll make room for the kid waiting for my table? Maybe.
But I've always been bad at leaving parties, looking up to see
it's just me and the sleepy hosts. Always afraid
I'll miss something: Phil passed out on the sofa
with a mascara goatee, Chuck making out with the new au pair,
Dolan singing "Running Bear." No, I won't ever agree to leave.

Old

A thousand yawns from now
when I am a bent question mark
and the children are busy living

and a push of a buzzer
summons the night nurse,
I will drag my oxygen tank trolley

resistant like a leashed mutt
across sticky linoleum
to peek between drawn blinds

and squint to find Orion,
the Big Dipper and Polaris
and remember a beach in Rhodes

where stars littered the sky
like luminescent river stones
so close

we could pluck them
from the heavens,
offer them to each other

and the universe
seemed – like our lives –
to roll on forever.

We had few questions
and the sky seemed full
of answers, some hurtling
like arrows into the future.

At the Museum of Medical Oddities

We fan out based on interest and strength of stomach.
A full cabinet of scrubbed skulls listing names, ages, occupations,
and dates of death seems harmless enough, but around the corner

a gangrenous hand, a cabinet of bones ravaged by syphilis,
and the Soap Lady – her body fat turned to a mottled wax now lying
in a clear glass coffin like a Madame Tussaud's heat casualty –

reveal the real scope of the operation. *It gets worse downstairs,*
Will says as he retreats to the lobby. *What am I doing here?*
It's a dead people freak show. How different

from reality TV with "little people" chocolatiers or houses full
of anorexics clawing each other for the modeling jackpot, or even
the jiggling of *American Idol*'s early rounds? I wince,

hating the voyeur in me. We should be at Betsy Ross'
or the Barnes' Museum or some nouveau-something bar
on the Philadelphia harbor instead of here

gawking at the bones of a seven-foot-six Kentucky giant
next to a skeleton of a three-foot-six female dwarf.
But something pulls me forward. Erin, Zak and I linger

at the mass murderer's brain and the victim's skull with an ax-size gap
until I'm brought to a halt at the cast of the original Siamese Twins
Chang and Eng across from their preserved livers. Their plaster selves

stand behind glass, the two of them turned at 90° angles
and all these preserved parts sharpen into a human focus.
As Erin studies row upon row of eyeballs afflicted

by everything from conjunctivitis to a cancer that protrudes
like a ping pong ball from its strained lids, and Zak shudders
at an enormous clogged human colon, I stare into the smooth eyes

of Chang and Eng. After death, doctors found only cartilage
held them together. Even the surgeons of their time could have split them.
But when Eng woke to find Chang dead beside him, he said, *No,*

to the doctor summoned to separate them, leaving the world
three hours after his still conjoined companion. And now
the carefully sliced human brains, the ossified ear bones

and the yellow, rubberish malformed babies perfectly preserved
in cloudy jars drive me upstairs. *How did you last that long?* Anne asks
as I stumble into the front lecture hall and begin to prattle on

about Chang and Eng. My kids, wife, niece Allie
all squeeze onto a dark wooden bench and listen distractedly.
Before us in the large room, rows of folding chairs

face a microphone and lectern prepared for a talk
about the telltale signs of fibrodysplasia ossificans progressiva
to real doctors who might be able to do something about it,

but hunger overcomes disgust and we go. I want to look again
into the calm, plaster eyes of Chang and Eng and say *Goodbye,*
but I'm pulled out the door by the same string that pulled me in

and as I hit the Philadelphia streets once walked by Rocky
and Springsteen and Ben Franklin, all I can think of is Chang and Eng
in a famous photo wearing a one-piece double tuxedo top,

holding their suit coats open to show off their black satin vests.
Later in a Chinese-Peruvian restaurant savoring my duck Bao Buns
and lump crab empanadas, the children debate the grossest exhibit

(The woman with the forehead horn and the 40-pound colon lose
to the two-headed baby in a jar) and I pull my shoulders back like Chang
and Eng, push my chest forward and look straight into the camera's eye.

Everybody's Vaguely Familiar

Four rows up in 27E I saw Judy Something (I started with A: Allison?
      Barbara? Carol?), a teacher from the middle school and her husband, Bill
(or Bob), my son's old principal. The silver-haired women in 31A and 31B
      might have bowled with my mom. We might have bumped behinds
on the dance floor at my wedding as the band played "All of Me."

Even the steward-flight attendant-whatever guy looks like a goateed
      version of my cousin Mark. I doubt he's left his wife and children,
but who knows? We've lost touch. Maybe he was afraid to tell me --
      afraid I'd disapprove. But Mark, It's okay. I could be you on another plane
or you could be me sitting here wondering if the guy stuffing a too big,

too green bag in the overhead is a taller, pock-marked Uncle Pete –
      if he put on thirty pounds. How identical we almost are. How subtle
the variations. I sit, hello smile ready, still nursing the light stomach
      of the plane's take-off, contemplating not just the unknown places I could go,
but the people I might have been – like the tanner, rounder me

I passed in 2B in sun-glasses, clad in black, with paint stains
      in the ridges of his knuckles. He could be the me who stayed in LA
thirty years ago returning now from some gallery opening
      or on-location background paint job, or just another visit
to my parole officer. And now, as a stewardess – a dead ringer

for Debra Winger – drags her cart and hands an aluminum-wrapped chicken
      to the pale bald man in 31D, I study his profile. We may have grown up
in the same county, he too may have won Best Camper at Camp Holy Cross
      or he may have a sister who taught my children Spanish. Below us,
the shadow of our plane crosses Iowa fields, squares of yellow

and green broken up by brown ribbons of river. The Spanish teacher's
      brother ponders the in-flight crossword. The way he taps his pen
against his teeth seems so familiar – like a relative maybe, like me.

Chicopee Falls, 1926

My father presses against the walls of Nanny's womb,
pausing before sliding into this world. Nanny flinches
from the doctor's icy stethoscope in the drafty house
as Pop waits in the living room, whiskey and cigar
ready for the doctor's call, he hopes, of "It's a boy!"

Eileen, now two and three quarters,
listens – her ear cupped to the hallway wall.
She's told Dad about Pop's drinking and gambling,
about the movie theater won in a poker game
and lost weeks later at a boxing match.

He's felt the steady rhythms of Nanny's long shifts
at the carpet factory and heard the doors slam
after Pop's empty days of door to door sales.
He vows not to cry. Not in the cold air of today.
Not ever. He vows to grow fast, move far.

Out the window, stubborn leaves cling to the elms,
a sliver of moon hangs in the November sky.
It's 1926. My father relaxes his pressure
against the walls of Nanny's womb, rolls over,
crosses his arms, closes his eyes, says "Ready."

Cemetery Ride

I like to ride my bike through Oak Lawn Cemetery at dusk after it's closed
    squeezing through the gap in the fence and feeling my heart beat faster
        as I race by the office knowing how embarrassing it would be at 55

to be arrested for trespassing, although seeing my name in the Police Blotter
    would liven up my dull reputation around town. Growing shadows of obelisks
        and angels reach across browning grass to snag the smaller gravestones,

pulling them into one grey monument. I don't feel haunted by lingering souls
    that once inhabited these names etched like smoke into polished stone
        or the pale crumbling bones beneath, but more amused that they hoped

to immortalize themselves with granite and marble. I don't even visit
    my own father's grave unless my mother wants birthday flowers planted
        and I plan to have my ashes spread across some as yet undetermined

beach or mountain pass. But I come here, religiously. When I was a teen
    the cemeteries in town were the only place to be alone to smoke cigarettes
        or make out with Megan Slater or drink Colt 45's and ass kickers

with Dave O & Jimmy Jackens or lie back, a slab of granite as our headboards,
    and search for shooting stars or make up our own constellations or just breathe
        and listen to our hearts synchronizing beneath our narrow rib cages.

I think I copped my first feel in a graveyard beneath a sliver of moon like this one
    rising out of the oaks. I wish now for a graveyard reunion with all those
        thirteen-year-olds who shared the need to *get out*, to *do* something,

sneaking out in the night to bump against each other, desperate to claim
    the world as our own. I pedal up the hilly paths startling deer venturing out
        as the shadows lengthen, pausing for a what-are-you-doing-here? stare

before scampering off despite my assurances I'm just passing through.
 I love these neat rows, cut stones in green grass, small furled flags,
  all the names, the birth dates and death dates, the sloppier pattern

of family mausoleums and Virgin Marys on the hills, the sound of my breath,
 the steady piston pumping of my knees, the whirring wheels. And
  as I stop for water by the Mill River, shallow now in August, snaking along

the cemetery's edge, I realize I want to spread my ashes from a plane at sunset
 over this very spot, falling like grey rain over some smooching teens or
  a middle-aged bicyclist looking up to the sky, saying *What the hell is that?*

Put Down This Poem and Call Your Mother

It's only now, four years gone that I see her clearly –
not the mute and creaky shadow of her at the end, breath shallow,
aides holding the phone to her ear as I read meaning
in each hesitation. No, the real her. But I can't hear her voice

mischievous as she feeds raccoons in the backyard oak,
or singing *tinkle tinkle little star* outside the bathroom door
as Zak, then four, peed. Or asking the obscene phone caller
if he was lonely. I can't hear her detailing the who-sat-with-who

at the senior home dinners or sightings of long forgotten neighbors
at the mall, her thin fingers twirling the cord we'd never fully cut.
I long to hear her inhale before a laugh, her long sigh,
the busy silence when she searched for topics.

"Hello, it's me," I'd say. "Hello, me," she'd answer,
her blue eyes an amused squint.

Drunken Santa

"That's Venus," Zak says, pointing to the bright light just to the right
        of the near-full moon. "And that?"
I point to a light to the left, before I realize it's moving. "A sleigh?" I ask.

But he's busy cataloguing the sky. His response to the chaos of the world
        is to order it; mine is to make fun.
The dog trots between us on Woods End Road. Zak names the planets

his voice now as deep as mine. He creates creatures from the constellations,
        stories out of the jumble;
we walk on – two Greek sailors navigating the dark Aegean.

Or one Greek sailor and a Greek jester making faces in the front of the boat.
        Charlie's white retriever coat glows
like a ghost in the darkness; his nose instinctively reads the pavement ahead.

I point to blow-up decorations on neighbors' lawns that during the day,
        without compressors pumping them
full of light and life, look like drunken Santas face-planted in the yard.

When four-year-old Zak told a friend that flat-toothed dinosaurs ate plants
        and sharp-toothed ones ate meat,
I asked about buck-toothed dinosaurs. He told his friend, "My dad's a joke."

"A joker," I corrected, but he'd already hustled the friend upstairs.
        "There's Orion," Zak says. "And there,
see the Bull's horns?" Freed from the smoky skies of Philly where he lives,

he points to Jupiter: "That's what the wise men saw over Bethlehem."
        He's as excited as twenty years ago
begging at bedtime to be quizzed on dinosaur names.

We enter the cemetery where a perimeter of oaks and thick firs
        give an undiluted view of the sky.
Zak mentions a book of star maps by the author of *Curious George.*

Each page is one night's constellations and I remember Curious George's bike
        and the bike
I tried to assemble for Zak one Christmas Eve, and the note I wrote from Santa.

"Dear Zak, This training wheel broke when your bike fell
        out of the sleigh.
Tell your dad to bring it Blinns to get it fixed."

I unleash Charlie and he lopes off, tail wagging, into the grass at the edge
        of the woods: zig zagging,
nose sniffing, assembling the story of the day like an archeologist of odors.

"That's Cassiopeia." Zak points north. On the hill, Zak points to Mars
        and the arcing belt where the planets
reveal themselves over the year. For a moment I can see patterns

everywhere: the stars, the rows of marble headstones converging toward
        a distant vanishing point,
their moonlit tops a string of hyphens or perhaps dots and dashes

sending a message from the dead. Charlie jigs and jags like a ghost dog
        scribbling some canine manifesto
across the grass. "And that," Zak points left of Cassiopeia, "is Drunken Santa."

"What?" I squint at the sky. "Just kidding," he says. But before I can laugh,
        he's returned to spinning and pointing
and naming, his tall silhouette sketching patterns on the anarchy of stars.

Perfectly Good Shoes

It started with a pair of desert boots I begged for seventh-grade Christmas
that arrived weeks after everyone stopped wearing them. I was spoiled.
A billion people in China were desert-bootless – I didn't care.
My mother started wearing them around the house, then for short trips to town.

Soon she added my discarded denim bellbottoms with red pinstripes,
my leather belt with the dancing bears buckle. My teen years were haunted
by mismatched versions of my old selves – my mother's pale, smiling face
perched on top. Even after I moved out, married, had kids, I never knew

what mishmash of my old tie-dyed T-shirts, disco shoes, madras shorts
or wide-collared floral shirts would show up at Easter or Fourth of July
along with news of successful classmates and clipped obits of neighbors
I never knew I'd known. When she died, I emptied her closets

and gave it all to a Greek church across town. But on cold mornings
I see the frayed arm of my Christmas sweater toss the paper on my lawn.
At night my tattered ninja pants take my movie ticket and tear it in half.
And my laced-together desert boots dangle from a wire downtown.

Acknowledgments

Grateful acknowledgment is made to the editors of the following publications in which the following poems, some in slightly different forms, first appeared.

- *2River View:* "In Praise of Heart Attacks" and "In Fear of Heart Attacks"
- *Barrow Street Review:* "Breaker 1-9"
- *The Chaotic Review:* "Writing Your Own Obituary"
- *Clackamas Literary Review:* "The Poetry Teacher"
- *Connecticut River Review:* "Counting," "How to Write a College Essay" and "The Body"
- *The Cortland Review:* "After the Funeral," "Signs" and "Old"
- *CWP:* "Granny's Yellow Plastic Radio"
- *Eunoia Review:* "Put Down This Poem and Call Your Mother"
- *The Fiddleback:* "At the Museum of Medical Oddities"
- *The Looking Glass:* "He couldn't remember"
- *NoiseMedium:* "Two Weeks After Judgment Day"
- *Poet Lore:* "Cemetery Ride"
- *Poetry Quarterly:* "How to Talk to Old People"
- *Rattle:* "Man on the Floor," "Holy Shitballs!" and "Rob Smuniewski is Dead"
- *Red Eft Review:* "Family Vacation 1965," "Chest Wounds" and "Everybody's Vaguely Familiar"
- *SNReview:* "Perfectly Good Shoes"
- *Southern Poetry Review:* "Donny One-Note"
- *The Southern Review:* "The God of Stupidity" and "Philtrum Guards"
- *Startle Us Anew:* "Carry/Miscarry"
- *Stirring: A Literary Collection:* "Bonehead," and "Summer Drunk"
- *The Westchester Review:* "Spittin' Image"

CPSIA information can be obtained
at www.ICGtesting.com
Printed in the USA
JSHW010734290120
3869JS00001B/31